ma⊙ic BULLET

10 SECOND RECIPES

AND

USER GUIDE

www.HomelandHousewares.com

FOR YOUR SAFETY, READ BEFORE OPERATION

- Read all instructions before operating the Magic Bullet.
- Do not immerse the cord, plug or base in water or other liquids.
- Do not pull, twist or mistreat the power cord.
- Avoid contact with moving parts.
- To avoid serious injury and product damage, keep hands and utensils away from the moving blades.
- Always unplug the base when cleaning or assembling.
- Always use your Magic Bullet on a clean, flat, hard, dry surface.
- Always completely assemble the blade and cup before placing on the Power Base.
- Never microwave with the blade still attached. Remove the blade and twist on a Shaker/Steamer Top.
- When microwaving, beware of steam and use an oven mitt to remove the hot cups from the microwave.
- Do not allow the cord to touch hot surfaces or hang over the side of the counter or table.
- Unplug the Magic Bullet when it's not in use, and before cleaning.
- Never leave the Magic Bullet unattended while it is in use.
- You risk personal injury, fire or electric shock if you use attachments, cups or parts other than those recommended by Homeland Housewares.
- Young children should not operate the Magic Bullet; older children should use only under direct supervision.
- The use of cups or any parts that were not designed to work with your Magic Bullet is not recommended and can result in injury.
- Never keep the blade running for more than one minute.
- Do not use the Party Mugs in the microwave.

Table of Contents

Table of Contents

THE MAGIC BULLET JUICER

Table of Contents

Table of Contents

Welcome

Congratulations on your purchase of the Magic Bullet, the personal, versatile countertop magician that works like magic. As you've no doubt noticed, the Magic Bullet is not your ordinary kitchen appliance. In fact, it's an entirely new concept in labor-saving devices. Unlike bulky blenders and unwieldy food processors that most of us only pull out of storage for specific recipes and special occasions, the Magic Bullet is so handy, so versatile and easy to use that you'll put it to work EVERY single day (probably several times a day). Best of all, it saves you time because it does almost any job in the kitchen in 10 seconds or less!

Peeling, chopping, mixing and blending are all tedious, time-consuming kitchen tasks that can really take the joy out of cooking, especially for those who are pressed for time. But with the Magic Bullet you can peel, chop, mix, blend, whip, grind and more — all in just seconds — for the fastest, tastiest meals ever. Imagine, everything from chopped onions and minced garlic to light and creamy cheesecake, all prepared in just 10 seconds or less! And that's just the beginning. The Magic Bullet cups are microwave safe, which means you can actually cook in them. Afterward, simply pop on one of the stay-fresh resealable lids to keep leftovers fresh and flavorful for days. Just think … no knives, cutting boards, or pots and pans to clean; no plastic wrap, foil or plastic storage containers to mess with. The Magic Bullet does it all. And because your Magic Bullet cups, Party Mugs, lids and blades go right in the dishwasher, cleanup is a breeze. So you save even more time!

Because the Magic Bullet is intended for everyday use, it has been designed to be compact so that it easily fits on any countertop, always right where you need it. And only the Magic Bullet comes with the ingenious accessories that turn it into the Bullet Blender, a full-size blender perfect for creating family-size batches of your favorite drinks, and the Bullet Juicer, ideal for turning fresh fruits and vegetables into delicious, nutritious juices the whole family will love.

We sincerely hope you enjoy using your Magic Bullet as much as we do. We're confident that it will soon become your favorite kitchen helper … one that you will use every day!

For your convenience we've created a series of icons to make it easy to find the appropriate recipe and blade attachment.

 Use the *Cross Blade* attachment

 Use the *Flat Blade* attachment

 Fat-Free

 Vegetarian

 Kid-Friendly

 Contains alcohol, act responsibly

 Travels well

 Caution

SAVE THESE INSTRUCTIONS
FOR HOUSEHOLD USE ONLY

High-Torque Power Base

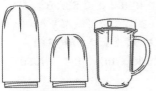

Tall Cup, Short Cup, Party Mugs

Cross Blade

Flat Blade

Magic Bullet Blender and Lid Attachment

Magic Bullet Juice Extractor Kit

 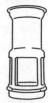

Plunger   Extractor

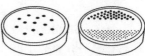

Shaker/Steamer Tops

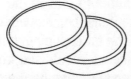

Stay Fresh Re-sealable Lids

Comfort Lip Rings

Order Optional Attachments

Before using your Magic Bullet for the first time, rinse all of the pieces, except for the *Power Base*, in warm soapy water. Rinse and dry well.

Tall Cup and Short Cup

These cups are used to mix, cook and store your ingredients. They are dishwasher-safe (top rack only) and microwave-safe.

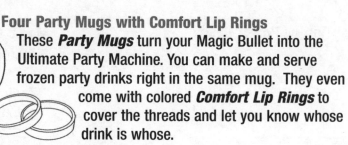

Four Party Mugs with Comfort Lip Rings

These **Party Mugs** turn your Magic Bullet into the Ultimate Party Machine. You can make and serve frozen party drinks right in the same mug. They even come with colored **Comfort Lip Rings** to cover the threads and let you know whose drink is whose.

*The Party Mugs are not microwave safe.

Power Base

The **Power Base** is the heart of the Magic Bullet. Simply place one of the **Bullet Cups** or **Party Mugs** onto the **High-Torque Power Base** and press. Nothing could be easier.

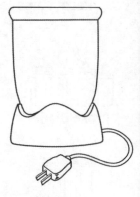

 Caution: Do not submerge the **Power Base** in water and always unplug the **Power Base** before cleaning it.

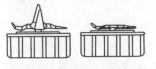

Cross Blade and Flat Blade

The Magic Bullet comes with two blades: a **Cross Blade** for chopping, grating and blending foods such as onions, cheeses, meats and frozen drinks, and a **Flat Blade** for whipping cream and grinding hard foods like coffee beans and spices. Both blades are dishwasher-safe. In the base of the blades, there is a plastic gasket that creates an airtight fit with the Magic Bullet cups. After washing a blade, check to make sure the gasket is still inside as the heat from some dishwashers can cause them to become loose.

Magic Bullet Blender and Lid

The full-size *Blender* attachment has all the power and capacity of an expensive, conventional blender, but the Magic Bullet's version only takes up as much counter space as a coffee mug. Use your *Magic Bullet Blender* anytime you need to whip up family-size batches of milkshakes, pancakes batters, or to make big batches of your favorite frozen cocktails at your next Bullet Bash. The *Blender Lid* comes with a pop-top for slipping in ingredients while the motor is running, mess-free.

Magic Bullet Juice Extractor Kit

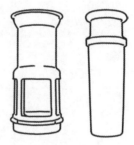

These two pieces, the *Extractor* and *Plunger*, transform your Magic Bullet into the *Magic Bullet Juicer* that does the same job as those large expensive juicers ... but unlike the big extractors, the *Magic Bullet Juicer* cleans up in seconds! Each piece is dishwasher-safe!

Shaker/Steamer Tops

Your Magic Bullet comes with two handy *Shaker/Steamer Tops* that are used for steaming foods in the microwave, or as shaker tops. The *Shaker/Steamer Top* with the large holes is for coarse ingredients such as Parmesan cheese, the other is for finely ground spices such as cinnamon or nutmeg.

Stay-Fresh Re-sealable Lids

With the Magic Bullet — your personal, versatile, countertop magician — you can prep, cook and store your food in the very same vessel. No plastic wrap or storage containers are needed to keep your leftovers fresh. Your Magic Bullet comes with two *Stay-fresh Re-sealable Lids* that fit right on to the *Short* and *Tall Cups*, and *Party Mugs* to keep your leftovers fresh for days.

*Only use the *Shaker/Steamer Tops* to heat food in the microwave.

Using the Magic Bullet

Using the Magic Bullet is as easy as 1, 2, 3 …

1. Load the ingredients into the *Short Cup*, *Tall Cup*, or *Party Mug*.

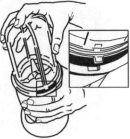

2. Twist on the *Cross*, or *Flat Blade* until the blade and cup have a tight seal.

3. Line up the tabs, place the bullet on the *Power Base* and press down on the cup to turn it on.

Here's how it works: As long as you're holding it down, the Magic Bullet is on. When you want the blades to stop, simply let go.

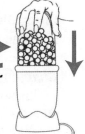

"Lock On" mode: For hands-free operation, press down and gently turn the cup clockwise until the tabs lock under the lip of the *Power Base*. Once you are in **Lock On** mode, the motor runs continually. To turn it off, simply twist the cup back counterclockwise and release the cup.

Caution

Never put your hands or utensils near the moving blades and never use your hands or utensils to press the activator buttons down while the *Power Base* is plugged in.

Caution

If the blade stops in Lock On mode, unplug the Magic Bullet immediately. Sometimes, especially when the motor is coming up to speed, a hard ingredient, such as a carrot chunk, can get stuck in the blade and stop it from turning. If the blade stops, UNPLUG THE MAGIC BULLET IMMEDIATELY. Take the blade/cup assembly off and give the ingredients a good shake to unblock the blade. If the blade still seems obstructed, twist off the blade and carefully (it's sharp) spin the blade manually. Once the blade will spin, plug the Magic Bullet back in and try again — you should be good to go.

Never run the Magic Bullet for more than one minute at a time, as it can cause permanent damage to the motor. If the motor stops working, unplug the ***Power Base*** and let it cool for a few hours before attempting to use it again. Your Magic Bullet has an internal thermal breaker that shuts the unit off when it overheats. Letting the thermal breaker cool down should allow it to reset.

Choosing the Right Blade

The Magic Bullet comes with two blades:

Cross Blade
The Magic Bullet ***Cross Blade*** is used for ...

Chopping — Foods like onions, garlic and carrots, and for making dips such as salsa, bean dip, or gazpacho.
Blending — The ***Cross Blade*** pulverizes ice for smoothies, frozen cocktails and milkshakes.
Mixing — Batters for pancakes, muffins and quick breads are mixed in seconds.
Grating — Foods like hard and soft cheeses and chocolate are grated in just seconds.
Pureeing — Dishes such as hummus, all-natural soups, and baby food are creamy smooth in seconds.
Shaving Ice and Frozen Fruits — For tasty treats such as snow cones or fruit sorbets.
Grinding Meats — Delicious chicken and ham salads or pâtés are ground in seconds.

Magic Bullet Techniques

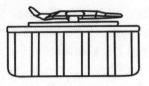

Flat Blade
The straight *Flat Blade* is used for…

Grinding and Chopping harder, single ingredient items such as:
coffee beans
nuts
cinnamon sticks
dried fruit

Or Whipping foods such as:
homemade whipped cream
cream cheese schmears
butter

Magic Bullet Techniques

The "Pulse" Technique

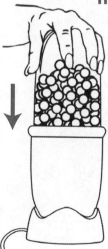

Because the Magic Bullet's motor is so powerful, if you aren't careful you can quickly overprocess food and turn it into mush. That is why when you want to make foods such as chunky salsa, or coarse chopped onions, the **Pulse** technique is key. **Pulsing** takes a tiny bit of getting used to, but once you get a feel for it, you'll be a Pro in no time!

To *Pulse* you simply press down on the cup very quickly and immediately release. For foods that you want coarsely chopped, a quick tap on the top of the cup is all you need. Then let the blades come to a complete stop and tap again until you get the consistene.

Using Your Magic Bullet

THE SECRET: The trick to successful **Pulsing** is to make sure that the machine doesn't accidentally slip into **Lock On** mode. To avoid this, simply use your other hand to apply counter-clockwise pressure on the cup as you **Pulse**.

To start ... hold the cup at the base and apply counter-clockwise pressure to it to keep it from locking on.

Then ... with your other hand, tap the top of the cup and immediately release. Continue **Pulsing** until you get the consistency you want.

The "Shake" Technique
Sometimes, when you are working with thicker ingredients, like those in chicken salad (Page 63) or marinara sauce (Page 67), the density of the mixture can make it hard for the ingredients toward the top of the cup to make it down to the blade. If some of your ingredients are having a hard time making it down to the blade, simply use this **Shake** technique.

The "Cocktail" Shake: When making smoothies, dips or other recipes where you are using the Bullet in **Lock On** mode, simply ...

While in Lock On mode ... pick up the whole cup and *Power Base* and shake it like a cocktail shaker.

Repeat ... if necessary until you achieve the consistency you want.

The "Shakin' Pulse": When you need to shake ingredients that you want coarsely chopped, like salsa or meat salads, you are going to want to use the **Shakin' Pulse** technique.

First ... Make sure the hand holding the cup is applying counter-clockwise pressure to keep it from locking on.

Then ... Give the Bullet a strong downward shake to throw the ingredients into the blade, and **Pulse** at the bottom of the shake.

Repeat ... until you get the right consistency.

The "Tap" Technique

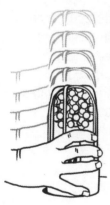

If you have a problem with sticky ingredients clinging to the side of the cup instead of being recirculated into the cutting zone ...

First ... Take the cup off the *Power Base* and *Tap* the cup and blade assembly on the counter to force the ingredients down into the blades.

Then ... Replace the cup and blade assembly to the *Power Base* and finish processing.

Chopping Onions and Garlic

With the Magic Bullet, chopping onions and mincing garlic is effortless. No more tears, no more stinky hands and no more knife and cutting board … you are literally seconds away from chopped, minced, even pureed onions and garlic.

First … prep the onions or garlic by removing any skin and making sure the pieces will fit into the Magic Bullet cup.

Next … Place the whole onions, onion pieces, or garlic into the *Short Cup* and twist on the *Cross Blade*.

Then … Give it several very quick **Pulses**. Remember to apply a bit of counter-clockwise pressure to the cup to keep it from locking on (see the **Pulse** technique on Page 15). With the other hand, give it a quick tap and release as soon as you hear the motor start. For coarser onion or garlic chunks, **Pulse** only a few times. For a minced consistency, **Pulse** five or six times. And for a smooth puree, just keep **Pulsing**, or **Lock On** (see Page 13) until you've achieved a smooth, thin consistency.

 When chopping onions and garlic, you may find the **Tap** Technique (Page 17) helpful.

Magic Bullet Basics

Smoothies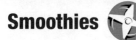

The Magic Bullet is perfect for creating delicious, satisfying, frosty smoothies and protein drinks. The best part is that you blend your ingredients and drink your smoothie out of the very same dishwasher-friendly cup … no mess! Plus, the power of the Magic Bullet pulverizes ice in a way few blenders ever will.

First … Add your favorite smoothie ingredients and ice into the *Tall Cup*, or *Party Mug*, and twist on the *Cross Blade*. (See recipes on Page 82.)

Then … Place the cup onto the *Power Base*, push down on the cup and twist clockwise until the tabs of the cup fit under the lip of the *Power Base* and the motor is running consistently (**Lock On** mode).

Keep blending … until you achieve a smooth consistency. The thickness of the drink will depend on the ingredients you use. You'll usually be able to hear when it's done. When all the ice is crushed, the grinding sound will stop and you'll hear a nice even whirring sound.

 If your smoothie is so thick that the ice or fruit is having a hard time reaching the blade, add more liquid and continue blending.

 Experiment with different smoothie ingredients. Smoothies are all about throwing whatever fruits, juices, yogurts, or whatever you have around the house, into a cup and giving it a whirl. Feel free to experiment with different ingredients and then share your masterpieces with us by posting them on the Magic Bullet website — **www.BuyTheBullet.com**.

Frozen Drinks

When it's frozen drink time your Magic Bullet is, hands down, the Ultimate Party Machine! Because the drinks are so quick and easy to make, everyone can have their favorite frozen cocktail. Plus, you can make the drinks right in the *Party Mugs*, then twist on your favorite-color *Comfort Lip Ring*, so everyone knows whose drink is whose. Partying has never been easier — or more fun!

First ... Add ice to the *Party Mug* (or *Tall Cup*).

Next ... add your favorite ingredients (see page 43 for some of our favorites) and twist on the *Cross Blade*.

Then ... Place the cup onto the *Power Base*, push down on the cup, twist to *Lock On* mode and blend until smooth.

Be Responsible ... Everyone at Homeland Housewares encourages you to have a great time, but please do so responsibly. Do not drink and drive, and please be careful when you are consuming alcohol.

 If your drink is so thick that the ice or fruit is having a hard time reaching the blade, add more liquid and continue blending.

Grinding Coffee

There is nothing better than a steaming cup of java made with freshly ground beans. Unfortunately, most bean-grinders are inconvenient and inevitably make a big mess on the countertop. Finally, with the Magic Bullet, grinding coffee is a breeze because you twist the blade off from the top, and the coffee is in the bottom of the cup. That means you don't have to go through that whole flipping-the-cup-over-to-get-the-coffee-out ordeal that you do with the typical bean-grinders. Plus, because all the Magic Bullet parts are washable, you can wash away the flavored coffee tastes. Never again will your French Roast taste like French Vanilla!

First ... Add coffee beans to the *Short Cup* and twist on the *Flat Blade*.

Next ... Place the cup onto the *Power Base*.

Now ... Pulse a few times, or **Lock On**, until the beans are ground to the desired texture.

Remember ... the finer the grind, the stronger the coffee. If you want a milder brew, stop **Pulsing** when the beans have the texture of coarse sand. If you're going for an espresso-like jolt, keep grinding until the beans become a fine powder.

Check out Page 77 for some of our favorite coffee recipes.

Mixing Batters and Breads

Finally, there's a way to make baked goods without all the stirring, whisking and chopping! The Magic Bullet makes the preparation and cleanup of baked goods a piece of cake. Pancakes, muffins, breads and more have never been faster — or fluffier! What we like to do is start with instant batter mixes and then make them fancy by adding tasty ingredients like nuts, cinnamon or apple to the batter. Since it's so quick, everyone can have the add-ins they like.

First ... Add the ingredients into the Magic Bullet *Tall Cup*, or *Blender*, depending on the size of the batch.
Then ... Blend the ingredients until smooth.
When using add-ins ... The power of the Magic Bullet will mince add-ins into tiny little pieces — which is great for flavor, but you

may want bigger, chunkier pieces as well. For example, when making blueberry muffins, we recommend that you add about half of the blueberries you intend to use in with the batter to be blended, then add the other half after the batter is blended. Just twist off the blade, add the whole berries, twist the blade back on and **Shake** cocktail shaker style a few times. That way you get fantastic blueberry flavor mixed right in with the batter, and delicious whole blueberries throughout the muffins for wonderful texture. You can use this technique with nuts, raisins, chocolate chips, whatever you desire.

Chopping Fresh Herbs

Finally, an effortless way to get all of the zesty, pungent flavor of fresh chopped herbs, without spending an hour at the cutting board. Now, in just seconds, you can make any meal taste like it was prepared by a gourmet chef.

First ... Add several sprigs of your favorite herb to the *Short Cup*.

Then ... Twist on the *Cross Blade* and give it several quick **Pulses**. Remember to apply a bit of counter-clockwise pressure to the cup to keep it from **Locking On** (see the **Pulse** technique on Page 15.)

Adding a pinch of fresh dill, parsley, chives, or basil over soups, mashed potatoes, salads — literally any dish you can think of — adds such zing to the flavor of the dish and just enough "chichi-ness" to make your family and guests feel like you've pulled out all the stops.

Grinding Spices

Now it's easy to spice up your life ... just use your Magic Bullet. No pre-ground spice can hold a candle to a freshly ground blend; you have no idea what you've been missing. In seconds you can have pancakes sprinkled with fresh cinnamon, or eggnog with a pinch of fresh, zesty nutmeg ... the possibilities are endless, mouth-watering and effortless. And with the ingenious *Shaker Tops*, you can serve right to the table. Bon appetit!

First ... Add your favorite fresh spice to the *Short Cup*.
Next ... Twist on the *Flat Blade* and grind until you've created a slightly textured powder.
Then ... Twist on the *Shaker/Steamer Top* with the two sets of small holes and sprinkle to your heart's content.

Tips *Seasoned Butters.* With almost no effort you can look like a culinary school graduate ... by whipping up a few seasoned butters. Just add chives, garlic, honey, mustard seed, whatever you like, to slightly softened butter and whip in your *Short Cup* with the *Flat Blade*. You'll create a spread that will make everyday bread and butter a five-star experience. Add a pat to the top of cooked fish, chicken or into soups ... brilliance!

Grating Cheeses

Chopping cheese is a time-consuming process, and pre-shredded cheese can be expensive. Now, with your Magic Bullet, you can effortlessly cut up cheese in less time than it takes to find your cheese grater. You can even twist a handy *Shaker/Steamer Top* onto the Magic Bullet cup and turn your Magic Bullet cup into a cheese shaker!

First ... Add your favorite cheese to the *Short Cup*.
Next ... Twist on the *Cross Blade* and grind until you've created a coarsely textured powder.
Then ... Twist on the large-holed *Shaker/Steamer Top*.

Grinding Meats

Until now, grinding meat required special equipment and a lot of effort. Now, with the Magic Bullet, you can grind meat for fresh sirloin burgers, meat sauces and party patés right in your Magic Bullet ... in just 10 seconds or less.

First ... Add the meat to the *Tall Cup* and twist on the *Cross Blade*.
Then ... Pulse (Page 15) until you get the consistency you want. Since meat is very dense, you may need to use the **Tap** technique (Page 17) to make sure every bit gets ground.

Deviled Ham. Check out the Deviled Ham recipe on Page 66 for a scrumptious ground meat recipe.

Whipping Cream

Light, fluffy, delicious whipped cream used to require a bowl, a whisk and a heck of a lot of elbow grease. Now with the Magic Bullet, it's never been easier, or faster, to create mountains of cloudlike whipped cream.

First ... Add heavy cream to the *Short Cup*.

Then ... Twist on the *Flat Blade* and whip until smooth. You'll hear it when it's done; the sound of the motor will change to a hum.

See the Magic Bullet coffee drinks section on Page 77 for a number of tantalizing coffee recipes that use whipped cream, or take a look at the dessert section on Page 72.

Cooking and Storing Leftovers

Cooking in the Magic Bullet Cups

Unlike conventional blenders or food processors, the Magic Bullet's job isn't done once the ingredients are blended. Once you've prepared your food, your Magic Bullet is then ready to cook it as well! Just remove the blade, twist on a *Shaker/Steamer Top* and place the cup in the microwave. Seconds later, you'll have steaming hot soups, rich and hearty pasta sauces or delicious melted cheeses, perfect for pouring over tortillas or vegetables, all without dirtying a dish, and with no pots and pans to clean!

First ... Blend or **Pulse** your ingredients together.

Then ... Remove the blade, twist on a *Shaker/Steamer top* (do not put the blades in the microwave) and place the cup in the microwave.

Cook until ready, then ... Remove with an oven mitt and serve.

Caution The single most important rule to remember for using the cups in the microwave: **Take off the blade!** The blades have metal in them and we all know that metal and microwaves don't mix. Never microwave food using the airtight lids, always use the *Shaker/Steamer Tops*. Also, remember that the contents and the cup will be hot, so always use an oven mitt.

Storing Leftovers in the Magic Bullet Cups

At Homeland Housewares, we understand that your time is valuable; that is why we've made *Stay-Fresh Re-sealable Lids* that twist right onto the Magic Bullet cups. Now you can prepare, cook and store your food all in the same vessel! No unnecessary dishes to clean, no plastic wrap, foil or plastic containers to deal with ... just twist on a stay-fresh lid and pop your leftovers in the refrigerator. You can even bring your leftovers to work or school, by just tossing the sealed cup into your bag and go! Then at work, you can reheat your leftovers in the microwave — all in the same cup!

Cleaning the Magic Bullet

Everyone hates cleaning up, which is just one more reason the Magic Bullet is so great. You can make and cook fresh homemade spaghetti meat sauce (see recipe on Page 67) from scratch and only use one tall Bullet cup! Imagine delicious, piping hot pasta sauces, salsa, fresh soups and more, all prepared with no cutting boards, no pots and pans, just a single cup and blade to put in the dishwasher. It doesn't get any easier than that.

 Always unplug the Magic Bullet when cleaning or assembling.

Washing Magic Bullet Attachments

It is so easy … Just place any of the pieces (except for the *Power Base*) on top shelf of the dishwasher, or hand wash with warm soapy water and rinse.

 Always make sure the gaskets are still inside after cleaning. The heat from some dishwashers can cause them to become loose and pop out.

 Stubborn cleanup When you let ingredients dry in the Magic Bullet, or when you've melted cheese in the cups, make your cleanup a snap by filling the cup with soapy water and microwaving it for one minute. That will loosen the stuck ingredients and with a light scrub, you'll be all done.

Cleaning the Magic Bullet Power Base

For the most part the *Power Base* doesn't really get dirty, but if you neglect to twist the blade onto the cup tightly, liquids can leak out and get into the base and activator buttons. Here's how to clean it up.

Easy Clean Up

Before you begin … The most important thing is to UNPLUG the *Power Base*!

Then … Use a damp rag to wipe down the inside and outside of the *Power Base*.

Sometimes the base gets so dirty … that the little white sliders that activate the Magic Bullet get sticky. This can cause the motor to continue to spin even after you've released the cup. When this happens, start by UNPLUGGING the *Power Base*.

Then … Double-check that you've UNPLUGGED the *Power Base*, and use a damp rag to soften up the gunk around the activators as you work the activator buttons up and down until they move freely again.

 NEVER SUBMERGE THE POWER BASE IN WATER OR PLACE IT IN DISHWASHER

 Never put your hands or utensils near the moving blade and never use your hands or utensils to press the activator buttons down while the Power Base is plugged in.

Magic Bullet Blender

When it's time to whip up big batches of foods like pancakes, milkshakes, or frozen drinks, the Magic Bullet Blender has all the power and capacity of those expensive, bulky blenders without taking up all that counter space. The **Blender Lid** has two pouring spouts, one for straining and one for pouring, and a pop-out top, so you can add ingredients as you blend. Plus, everything is dishwasher-safe (top rack only), so cleanup is fast and easy.

Assembling the Magic Bullet Blender

Just ... Twist the **Cross Blade** onto the bottom of the blender pitcher.

Then ... Place the blender on the Magic Bullet base.

Using the Magic Bullet Blender

The Magic Bullet Blender is just like regular blenders, without all the confusing buttons.

Simply ... Place the assembled **Blender** onto the Power Base.

Then ... Push down on the **Blender** and twist clockwise until the tabs lock under the lip of the **Power Base** (**Lock On** mode).

And ... Put on the **Blender Lid** and blend.

Never run the Magic Bullet for more than one minute at a time, as it can cause permanent damage to the motor. If the motor stops working, unplug the **Power Base** and let it cool for a few hours before attempting to use it again. Your Magic Bullet has an internal thermal breaker that shuts the unit off when it overheats. Letting the thermal breaker cool down should allow it to reset.

Magic Bullet Juicer

Now you can make freshly squeezed juice every day of the week, at home, without all of the added sugar found in many store-bought juices and without the mess and big production that comes with most traditional juicers. In the *Magic Bullet Juicer*, making delicious, nutritious fresh juices like orange or pineapple, and instant energy cocktails is a snap.

Assembling the Magic Bullet Juicer

First ... Twist the *Cross Blade* onto the bottom of the *Blender*.

Then ... Insert the *Extractor* down the center of the *Blender* making sure to line the three notches up with the three ribs on the inside of the *Blender*.

Next ... Place the lid onto the *Blender* and align either the straining pourer or regular pourer up to the spout. Make sure the lid is locked on, it holds the *Extractor* insert in place.

And then ... Place the *Blender* on the Magic Bullet base.

Using the Magic Bullet Juicer

Before you begin ... Select your juice ingredients, make sure they are sized to fit into the *Extractor* and place them within arms reach of your *Magic Bullet Juicer*.

When you're ready to start juicing ... Remove the pop-top from the lid of the *Blender*, place the assembled *Magic Bullet Juicer* onto the *Power Base*, press down and turn the *Blender* clockwise until it is running in hands-free **Lock On** mode. *To avoid jamming the blades, which can cause serious motor damage, make sure the motor is running BEFORE you add any ingredients into the juicer.*

Then ... Place ingredients through the pop-top, down the center of the *Extractor*.

Push the ingredients ... down into the blade with the *Plunger* tool. The juice will accumulate in the pitcher around the *Extractor* insert.

Then ... Pour the juice into a glass with the juicer assembled as is, without removing or jostling the *Extractor*. Notice how the juice is on the outside of the *Extractor* and the pulp is on the inside? You need to be careful to keep the juice separate from the pulp. Pour the juice out carefully.

Caution *If the blade stops in Lock On mode, unplug the Magic Bullet immediately*. Sometimes, especially when the motor is coming up to speed, a hard ingredient, such as a carrot chunk, can get stuck in the blade. If the blade stops, UNPLUG THE MAGIC BULLET IMMEDIATELY and clear the blade before proceeding. Running the machine when the blades are obstructed can ruin the motor.

Notes Never run the Magic Bullet for more than one minute; it can cause permanent damage to the motor. If you still want more juice after 60 seconds of juicing, simply stop for a few seconds, then continue for another minute. If you do overheat the motor and it stops, unplug the *Power Base* and let it rest for a few hours before attempting to use it again.

10 Second Recipes

Our team at Homeland Housewares has had the pleasure of personally testing every single recipe suggestion in this cookbook. Out of the thousands of delicious delicacies you can prepare in the Magic Bullet, we've chosen our favorite "10 seconds or less" recipes to share with you. We've added our notes, serving suggestions and tips so you can get the most out of each recipe.

The Magic Bullet is all about creating delicious meals, drinks and snacks in 10 seconds or less, with virtually no clean up. During our recipe creation and selection process, we discovered certain ingredients made the 10 second recipes even easier, faster and neater. Here they are:

Boiler Onions
Boiler onions are flavorful little onions that are about an inch to an inch and a half in diameter. You can find them in the produce section of most grocery stores. They are perfect for the Magic Bullet because you can throw them in whole, no cutting board, no knife ... just toss them in the Magic Bullet cup and you're ready to go. One boiler onion (they range in size) is the equivalent of about 1/4 cup of onion.

Pre-peeled Garlic In Jars
Some genius decided to pre-peel garlic and sell it in jars. You can find this pre-peeled garlic in the produce section of most grocery stores. When a recipe calls for a clove or two of garlic, just open up the jar and toss them in the cup. All the flavor, without all the work...it doesn't get any easier!

Cherry Tomatoes
Cherry tomatoes are not only perfectly sized to throw right into the Bullet Cups, they are extremely flavorful. Our recipes are based on the cherry tomatoes that are about an inch in diameter. On average about 4-6 cherry tomatoes equals a 1/4 cup of tomato.

Baby Carrots

Cutting and peeling carrots is tough work. We highly recommend using the pre-peeled, baby size carrots that are available in the produce section of most grocery stores. These tiny carrots are sweet, tasty and perfectly sized for the Magic Bullet cups.

And remember, to make things as easy as possible for you, we've created a series of icons so, in a glance, you can learn about a recipe. The key of icons used in this book can be found on page 8.

For your convenience, we've also created an index that categorizes the recipes by Fat-Free, Kid-Friendly and more. The index can be found on Page 91.

We want you to try the recipes in this cookbook because, well, we've devoured every one of them and know how good they are! We also want to make sure you understand that with The Magic Bullet, the possibilities are endless. Because everything is so quick and easy to make, it's the perfect device for experimenting.

Don't hesitate to add or omit ingredients and if you want to vary a recipe, or totally rework it … go for it. We encourage that type of Magic Bullet bravery. Go ahead and create your very own Magic Bullet masterpieces and when you are ready to share them with the rest of the world, you can post them on the Magic Bullet website at www.BuyTheBullet.com.

Party Dips

Why spend a fortune on mediocre store-bought dips when you can make your own tantalizing party spreads in less than 10 seconds, and for a fraction of the price. Each of these dips has been selected for flavor, popularity and ease. Go ahead and call some friends, it's time to throw a Bullet Bash!

Seven-Second Salsa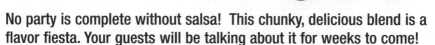

No party is complete without salsa! This chunky, delicious blend is a flavor fiesta. Your guests will be talking about it for weeks to come!

> 1-2 boiler onions or 1/4 of a regular sized onion (about 1/4 cup)
> 1/6 to 1/4 of a jalapeno pepper
> 8-10 cherry tomatoes or 1 regular size tomato (about 1/2 cup)
> 1-2 cloves garlic
> small sprigs of cilantro (optional)
> salt and pepper to taste

First ... Place all ingredients, in the order they are listed, into the *Tall Cup*. (You may have to cut the tomatoes a bit, depending on the size you choose.)

Then ... Twist on the *Cross Blade* and place the cup onto the *Power Base*.

Next ... Give it several quick **Pulses**. Salsa should be chunky, so be careful not to over-process it. Remember to apply a bit of counter-clockwise pressure to the cup to keep it from **Locking On** (See **Pulse** technique on Page 15).

Repeat the quick Pulse technique ... until you achieve a blended yet chunky texture.

Party Dips

 When you pour your fresh salsa in a bowl, you may notice the power of the Magic Bullet has made it a little foamy. Don't panic — the foam is actually tiny air bubbles that go away after a few minutes. If it bothers you, lay a paper towel down on top of the salsa and gently blot ... no more foam. Also, when you make salsa with a knife, you typically seed the tomatoes first. Since we're throwing the tomatoes in whole, there may be more juice than you're used to. If so, just twist on the *Shaker/Steamer Top* and strain out some of the extra liquid.

 Serve your salsa with tortilla chips, slices of Italian bread, or as a dip for triangles of quesadilla (see recipe Page 41).

💡 *Chunkier Salsa.* For even chunkier salsa, after you're done **Pulsing**, stir in some canned (drained) black beans and a bit of canned corn — a fiesta for the taste buds!

Hallelujah Hummus

We love hummus because it's so rich and creamy! This traditional Greek delicacy can be served as a dip or a side dish.

> 1⁄4 cup chicken (or vegetable) stock
> 14 oz. can chickpeas (garbanzo beans),drained
> 3 cloves garlic
> 2 Tbs. lemon juice
> 3 Tbs. tahini (sesame paste)

First ... Add all ingredients into the *Tall Cup*.
Next ... Twist on the *Cross Blade* and blend until smooth.
Then ... Salt and pepper to taste.

Hummus is best served cold, with warm triangles of pita bread. The traditional way to serve it is to pour the hummus into a bowl and drizzle it with olive oil, then sprinkle the top with paprika.

Fat-Free Hummus

Dig in and enjoy this delicious hummus without worrying about your waistline!

> splash of fat-free chicken (or vegetable) broth
> 1 drained 14 oz. can chickpeas (garbanzo beans)
> 2 Tbs. lemon juice
> 2 cloves garlic
> sprinkle of paprika
> salt and pepper to taste

First ... Add all ingredients except for paprika into the *Tall Cup*.
Next ... Twist on the *Cross Blade* and blend until smooth.
Then ... Salt and pepper to taste, and sprinkle with paprika.

Hummus is best served cold, with warm triangles of pita bread.

Before-You-Know-It Bean Dip

Not all bean dip comes out of that creepy little can. You can make hearty, delicious, all-natural bean dip in seconds.

Dips

> 1 (15 oz.) can black beans, drained
> 1/4 of a medium-sized onion
>   (about 1/4 cup)
> 1-2 cloves garlic
> 1/4 cup roasted red peppers (jarred)

1/4 cup (fat-free) chicken or vegetable broth
2 Tbs. balsamic vinegar
dollop of sour cream (optional)
cayenne pepper to taste (optional)

First ... Drain most of the liquid out of the canned beans.
Then ... Load all the ingredients, in the order they are listed, into the *Tall Cup*.
And ... Twist on the *Cross Blade* and quickly **Pulse** (Page 15) until you reach the desired consistency.

This dip is great, either chunky or smooth. If you want it chunky, don't overdo the **Pulsing**. Quickly **Pulse**, stop and let the ingredients settle. Use the **Tap** technique (Page 17) to speed up the settling process. **Pulse** again and repeat until you've created the bean dip of your dreams!

This dip is great both warm and cold. If you go for the warm version, try adding 1/4 cup of cheddar cheese to the ingredients before you blend it. (If you don't have room, partially mix the ingredients, then add the cheese.) Take the blade off, place the *Shaker/Steamer Top* on the cup and microwave for about 2-3 minutes (until warm throughout). Give the dip another quick **Pulse** or two, then serve immediately. The warm version goes perfectly with nachos or sliced crusty Italian bread.

Use your favorite type of bean. Black beans can be substituted with pinto beans, white beans, whatever you're into.
Black bean sauce Add a cup of broth, then microwave to make a perfect sauce for pouring over chicken or fish.
Black bean soup Add a cup of broth, then microwave to make a zesty, flavorful soup — a great way to use any leftover dip. Throw in a few shrimp for a real treat.

Speedy Guacamole

A little guacamole trivia: During Super Bowl 2002, football fans consumed 13.2 million pounds of guacamole. Don't deprive your guests! With this simple, delicious recipe it's easy to give the gift of guacamole.

> 2 avocados
> 2-3 cloves garlic
> squeeze of lemon or lime juice (optional)
> 1 boiler onion or 1/4 of a regular sized onion (about 1/4 cup)
> 4-6 cherry tomatoes or 1/2 regular size tomato (about 1/4 cup)
> 1-2 sprigs of fresh cilantro
> 1/6 of a jalapeño pepper (optional)
> salt and pepper to taste

First ... Scoop out the meat of the avocados, discarding the pit, and place it in the *Short Cup*.

Next ... Place the remaining ingredients, in the order they are listed, into the *Short Cup*. (You may have to cut the tomatoes a bit, depending on the size you choose.)

Then ... Twist on the *Cross Blade* and place the cup onto the *Power Base*.

And ... Give it 3 or 4 quick **Pulses** until all the ingredients are chopped and blended. Make sure to apply a bit of counter-clockwise pressure to the cup to keep it from **Locking On**.
(See **Pulse** technique on Page 15.)
Since guacamole is thick, you may need to use the **Tap** technique (Page 17) to make sure everything gets completely chopped.

Serving Suggestion Guacamole tastes best when it's chilled. Serve with nachos, as a taco or fajita topping, or add a dollop to the top of a juicy burger and dig in. Mm-mmm!

Tips ***Not everyone likes tomatoes and onion in guacamole —*** feel free to omit them if you'd like. Or if you like tomatoes and don't have any fresh ones around the house, you can use canned tomatoes.

Appetizers

Who needs a caterer when you can do it by yourself in 10 seconds or less? From breathtaking stuffed mushrooms to zesty chicken quesadillas, your guests will think you're a culinary wizard when you create any one of these quick and easy masterpieces.

Suddenly Stuffed Mushrooms

What is it that makes stuffed mushrooms so special? We don't know for sure, but we do know these puppies will be gone before you can blink an eye. Do your guests a favor — make two batches. Scrumptious!

> 10-12 large mushrooms
> 1/4 cup Ricotta cheese
> 1/2 cup fresh spinach
> 1 oz. Parmesan cheese
> 1 clove garlic
> 1 boiler onion or 1/4 of a regular sized onion (about 1/4 cup)
> splash of chicken (or vegetable) broth

Before you begin ... Preheat the oven to 350 degrees.

Start off by ... popping off the stems off of the mushrooms, making an area for the stuffing in the mushroom top.

Then ... Load all the ingredients, except for the mushrooms, in the *Short Cup* and twist on the *Cross Blade*.

Pulse until ... the consistency is slightly textured, but not quite smooth.

And ... Spoon the mixed ingredients into the mushroom tops and cook on a lightly greased baking sheet for 15-20 minutes.

Appetizers

This recipe fills about 10-12 mushrooms. If you want to make more, simply double the ingredients.

 This recipe is the standard stuffed mushroom recipe. Feel free to add crab meat, crumbled bacon, lobster, whatever your heart desires into this mix and you'll have scrumptious stuffed mushrooms that will have your guests swooning!

Nanosecond Nachos

"Na-cho" average appetizer; everyone loves nachos! A perfect party opener that's quick, easy, inexpensive and delicious. What more can be said about this party favorite?

> 1 cup cheddar (or your favorite) cheese
> 1/4-1/2 of a jalapeño pepper

First ... Load the ingredients into the ***Short Cup*** and **Pulse** a few times (you want the jalapeños to keep a little bit of chunky texture).
Then ... Twist off the blade, and twist on a ***Shaker/Steamer Top***.
Microwave ... on high for about 1 1/2 minutes, until cheese is fully melted.
Pour ... over tortilla chips. Serve immediately.

 You can add anything you want to the top of your nachos. Guacamole, sour cream, black beans, tomatoes — even leftover chicken — are sure crowd-pleasers.

 Cup cleaning made even easier! When it's time to clean your ***Tall Cup***, fill it 3/4 full with hot water, then microwave for 45 seconds. That will re-melt the cheese, making cleanup a breeze.

Badda-Bing Badda-Boom Garlic Bread

Homemade garlic bread has never been easier, or more flavorful. The perfect blend of butter, cheese and garlic in every bite ... a real treat for the taste buds!

    1/2 cup butter or margarine
    2-3 garlic cloves
    1 oz. Parmesan cheese
    loaf of Italian (or French) bread

First ... Add butter or margarine to your *Short Cup* and screw on *Shaker/Steamer Top*.

Then ... Heat in the microwave unit the butter is melted, add garlic and cheese, then twist on *Cross Blade*.

Blend until ... smooth and spread down the middle of a loaf of crusty Italian or French bread. (Cut it down the center, lengthwise.)

And ... Toast open-faced until warm, then slice and serve!

Quickie Chicken Quesadilla

Interested in a nutritious lunch — or dinner — your kids will love? How about one that takes only seconds and has virtually no cleanup? This warm and cheesy Mexican favorite is perfect for kids, sports nights, snacks ... anytime. Dee-licious!

    2/3 cup cheddar (or your favorite)
        cheese
    1/2 cup cooked chicken
    4-6 cherry tomatoes or 1/2 regular
        size tomato (about 1/4 cup)
    2 flour or corn tortillas

Start by ... Adding all ingredients except for the tortillas into the *Tall Cup* and twist on *Cross Blade*.

Next ... Pulse your ingredients (see **Pulse** Technique on page 15) being careful not to slip into **Lock On mode**. Because the ingredients are thick, you may want to use the **Tap** technique on page 17.

Repeat the quick Pulse technique ... until you achieve a blended but chunky texture.

Spread the mixture ... between the tortillas and heat in microwave (high) for 1 1/2 minutes, until fully heated.

 Tips

Use your leftovers You can use any kind of leftover chicken you have, bbq, fried chicken, it all tastes great. Or, replace the chicken with ground beef, luncheon meats or any other left over meats you may have.

Omit chicken and replace with veggies Veggie quesadillas are just as delicious. Just add your favorite vegetables, like squash, onions and peppers, and dig in.

Frozen Adult Drinks

From fancy brunches to poolside frat parties, your Magic Bullet has you covered. This soup-to-nuts frozen drinks section has every recipe you need to impress everyone, from the stuffiest of stuffed shirts to the hardest of hardcore partiers.

Your Magic Bullet *Party Mugs* are the ultimate party tool: Not only can you blend and serve drinks in the same cup, you just twist on one of the colored *Comfort Lip Rings* and the different colors let you know whose drink is whose. No mess, no cleanup, no problems. Or, if you want to make big batches of frozen cocktails, just use the *Magic Bullet Blender* and you're seconds away from several servings of your favorite concoction.

And remember, your friends at Homeland Housewares are all about having a good time, but we want you to be safe about it. Please drink responsibly. Assign a designated driver and have a ball, but be careful!

Easy Frozen Margarita

It's no mystery why the frozen margarita is the country's most popular party drink. This frosty, thirst-quenching cocktail has just the right amount of bite to be absolute cocktail perfection. Bottoms up!

> ice
> 4 oz. margarita mix
> 2 oz. tequila

Step 1: Fill a *Party Mug* or the *Tall Cup* with ice.
Step 2: Pour in all of the ingredients.
Step 3: Blend until smooth.

Frozen Drinks

Frozen Adult Drinks

Easy Strawberry Frozen Margarita

Tangy and sweet, all together in one delicious, refreshing concoction. So divine, you'll surely want another.

ice
4 oz. margarita mix
2 oz. tequila
3-4 fresh or frozen strawberries

Step 1: Fill a *Party Mug* or the *Tall Cup* with ice.
Step 2: Pour in all of the ingredients.
Step 3: Blend until smooth.

Easy Watermelon Frozen Margarita

A refreshing and flavorful twist on the regular frozen margarita, this blend is perfect for brunches and poolside festivities.

ice
4 oz. margarita mix
2 oz. tequila
1 cup seeded watermelon

Step 1: Add the watermelon to a *Party Mug* or the *Tall Cup*.
Step 2: Fill the rest of the *Party Mug* or *Tall Cup* with ice.
Step 3: Pour in all of the remaining ingredients.
Step 4: Blend until smooth.

Make a *Peach Margarita* by adding 1 cup of peaches instead of the watermelon.

For super frosty Watermelon Margaritas, cut and freeze seeded watermelon cubes and use them as ice ... Mmm.

The only difference between margaritas and daiquiris is whether you use tequila or rum. Just replace the tequila with rum in any of the margarita recipes and you'll have a fruit-flavored daiquiri.

Classic Frozen Margarita

We know you're out there, the type that's constantly striving to make the best possible margarita. Here's a good starting place, then explore other concoctions; the possibilities are endless.

    ice
    1 1/2 oz. tequila
    1 oz. fresh lime juice
    1/2 oz. triple sec (or Cointreau)
    1 tsp. sugar (optional)

Step 1: Fill the 1/3 of the *Party Mug* or *Tall Cup* with ice.
Step 2: Add all other ingredients.
Step 3: Blend until smooth and slushy.

When you do create your perfect margarita, find it in your heart to share it with the rest of us. Please post your recipe on the Magic Bullet website at www.BuyTheBullet.com

Easy Frozen Daiquiri

Bring a little of Vegas' Flamingo Hotel into your own back yard — nothing says "kick up your heels, Vegas-style" more than a strawberry daiquiri.

    ice
    4 oz. daiquiri mix
    2 oz. light rum

Step 1: Fill a *Party Mug* or the *Tall Cup* with ice.
Step 2: Pour in all of the ingredients.
Step 3: Blend until smooth.

To make a **Strawberry Daiquiri** add a handful of fresh or frozen strawberries before blending.
To make a **Diva Daiquiri** add 1 oz. coconut rum before blending.
To make a **Purple Haze** add 1/2 oz. Blue Curacao before blending.
To make a **Derby Daiquiri** add 2 Tbs. fresh orange juice before blending.

Frozen Pina Colada

Every day is like an island getaway when you drink pina coladas. Created in Puerto Rico, this delicious blend of coconut and pineapple became a hit when the "Pina Colada song" reached the Top 40 in the '70s

> ice
> 2 oz. rum
> 1 good splash of cream of coconut
> 1 good splash of pineapple juice

Step 1: Fill a *Party Mug* or the *Tall Cup* with ice.
Step 2: Pour in all of the ingredients.
Step 3: Blend until smooth.

To make an **Easy Pina Colada**, just pick up some pina colada mix and blend with rum and ice.

A Bullet to the Head

The name says it all. Drink with caution and be sure to have a designated driver!

    ice
    1 oz. vodka
    1 oz. light rum
    1 oz. tequila
    1 oz. gin
    1 1/2 oz. sweet and sour mix
    3 oz. cola

Step 1: Fill a *Party Mug* or the *Tall Cup* with ice.
Step 2: Pour in all of the ingredients.
Step 3: Blend until smooth and serve.

Boulevard Bellini

A unique frozen version of the snazzy, upscale Bellini. A delicious blend of fruity flavor that's tasty without being sweet. A perfect cocktail for brunches and luncheons, or poolside, or breakfast, or anytime!

    ice
    frozen peaches
    2 shots champagne
    2 shots peach schnapps
    1 oz. lemon-lime soda
    1 tsp. sugar

Step 1: Fill a *Party Mug* or *Tall Cup* halfway up with ice and add frozen peaches to fill the cup.

Frozen Drinks

Step 2: Pour in all of the liquid ingredients.
Step 3: Blend until smooth.

Mystic Martini

Martini connoisseurs will be blown away by the ice slivers in this masterpiece. Not only that, the blending makes a spectacular, mystic display.

>   2 oz. gin or vodka
>   splash of dry vermouth
>   1 ice cube

Step 1: Add all the ingredients into the tall cup and **Pulse** until the ice is almost gone (a few small slivers is the goal).
Step 2: Pour into a martini glass.
Step 3: Garnish with an olive or cocktail onion.

Most people skip breakfast not because they don't want it, but because they don't have time. Finally, with the Magic Bullet, you can create a hearty, satisfying breakfast without fear of being late for work and without coming home to dirty dishes. In seconds you can mix up fluffy egg dishes, piping hot muffins, breads, pancakes ... you name it. Plus, cleanup is as simple as opening the dishwasher and popping in a few items — a great way to start the day.

In-a-Jiffy Flapjacks

With the Magic Bullet, making pancakes is so quick and easy, everyone can have their favorite kind. Start by mixing up the basic pancake batter, then add whatever ingredients your heart desires. You can create delicious blueberry, fluffy apple cinnamon, and hearty banana nut pancakes all from the same basic pancake batter and all in just seconds ... so everyone gets to enjoy exactly the type of pancakes that they're in the mood for.

> 1 cup milk
> 1 egg
> 1 cup pancake mix (Bisquick or any baking mix)

First ... Add milk and egg (or whatever ingredients your pancake mix requires) into the *Tall Cup*, then add pancake mix.
Next ... Give the ingredients several quick **Pulses** until the batter is blended. (Do not overprocess or pancakes can get tough.)
Then ... Pour 1/4 cup portions of batter onto a greased griddle/frying pan and cook over medium heat until the edges look dry, then flip and cook the other side until golden.

If you're feeding a crowd, double, triple or quadruple the recipe and use the *Blender* attachment for mixing — you can pour the batter right onto the griddle!

 Add a banana, a dollop of applesauce or a handful of berries to the mix before you blend ... divine!
Make your own spectacular **Fruit Syrup** by adding a handful of frozen (or fresh) fruit to the *Short Cup* and blend with the *Cross Blade* until smooth. If you want it warm, microwave for 30 seconds. If you want it sweet, add a teaspoon of sugar.

Blueberry Pancakes

First ... Throw a handful of frozen or fresh blueberries into the basic pancake recipe (above) and give a few quick **Pulses** to blend the batter and the blueberries.

Next ... Unscrew the top and add another small handful of whole blueberries, twist the lid back on and shake them together. (You don't want to blend again. The idea here is to mix some whole blueberries into the blueberry-flavored batter.)

Then ... Pour 1/4 cup portions of batter onto a greased griddle/ frying pan and cook over medium heat until the edges look dry, then flip and cook the other side until golden.

Almost-Makes-Itself Omelet

Remember when making an omelet required knives and cutting boards, multifarious bowls and a whole lot of chopping? Those days are over. Now with almost no effort, you can enjoy this hearty flavorful meal for breakfast lunch or dinner. With the Magic Bullet you chop the veggies, grate the cheese and whip the eggs all at the same time — all in less than 10 seconds! This recipe starts with the basic omelet recipe, then gives a variety of common omelet types to choose from. You don't have to limit yourself to these recipes — experiment and have a good time. Mix and match ingredients that appeal to you. Then follow the directions for either the "Easy Omelet" or the "Traditional Omelet". Bon appetit!

Basic Omelet Ingredients

3 eggs
splash of milk (cream, or water)
salt and pepper to taste

Popular Omelet Types

Ham and Cheese
2 oz. ham
1oz. cheddar and/or Colby Jack cheese

Hawaiian
2 oz. ham
pineapple
2 mushrooms
1/4 cup fresh tomato
1 oz. Monterey Jack cheese

Vegetarian
mushrooms
bell peppers
onions
tomato

Western
diced ham
bell peppers
onions
Monterey Jack cheese

The Easy Omelet

Instead of the typical stuffed omelet, this easy-to-make version uses the power of the Magic Bullet to fully integrate the ingredients within your omelet mixture, so every forkful is simply bursting with flavor. No matter what kind of omelet you're in the mood for, you'll be eating like a king in no time at all, with virtually no cleanup.

Before you start ... mixing your ingredients in the Magic Bullet, put a little oil or butter in a frying pan and let it start to heat up over medium heat. It only takes a minute or two, so don't start it too early.
Now ... Add the basic omelet and any additional ingredients in to the *Short Cup* and **Pulse** (see **Pulse** Technique on Page 15) until the ingredients are chopped.
Next ... Pour the omelet mixture into the heated, oiled frying pan.
Then ... Set the heat to medium low, put the cover on and cook until the omelet is set.
You might want to ... Use a spatula to pull a corner of the omelet back, letting any stubborn, uncooked egg roll over to the empty area of the frying pan.

The Traditional Omelet

If you're the type that likes to have the ingredients folded into the middle of your omelet, this preparation style is for you. You've never had a lighter, fluffier omelet! Enjoy!

Before you start ... mixing your ingredients in the Magic Bullet, put a little oil or butter in a frying pan and let it start to heat up over medium heat. It only takes a minute or two, so don't start it too early.
Then ... Add the basic omelet ingredients in to the *Short Cup* and whip until everything is mixed together.
And ... Pour the basic mixture into a heated, oiled frying pan. Set the heat to medium low and put the cover on.
Now ... **Pulse** a few times (see **Pulse** Technique on Page 15). Maintain a chunky texture.
And ... When your omelet looks set, add your filling mixture to one

side of the omelet and fold the other side over. Heat the omelet for a few more minutes until the filling is warm and serve immediately.

Tips *For an even easier omelet,* there are microwave-safe omelet cookers available in most department stores. You just pour in your Easy Omelet mixture and pull your fresh, flavorful, steaming hot omelet out of the microwave when it beeps. It doesn't get any easier!

For a low-fat version, simply use fat-free cooking spray to grease the frying pan.

For an even lower-fat version, use **egg whites** only.

Six-Second Scrambled Eggs

This simple recipe makes the fluffiest, most flavorful eggs you've ever tasted. You'll think you've died and gone to Heaven. No bowls, no chopping, no mess!

> 2 eggs
> splash of milk, cream, or water
> salt and pepper (optional)
>
> **Popular Additions**
> 1/2 oz. of your favorite cheese
> tomato wedge
> onion slices
> 1 oz. ham
> 2 basil leaves
> Whatever else your heart desires!

First ... Blend ingredients in the *Short Cup* and pour into a greased frying pan.

Then ... Stir until cooked and serve immediately.

Notes This recipe is for a single serving of scrambled eggs. Simply multiply the ingredients by the number of people you are going to serve ... Use the *Tall Cup* for more than two servings and if you're feeding an army, use the blender attachment for mixing.

Tips ***Super easy scrambled eggs*** For the **World's Easiest Scrambled Eggs**, follow the directions above and then microwave the egg mixture for 2-3 minutes. Pour the egg mixture in a bowl, or cook your eggs right inside the Magic Bullet cup! For perfect scrambled egg texture, once you can see the eggs are firming up, give the eggs a stir every 20 seconds or so ... simply divine with no mess. A hearty, effortless breakfast the kids will love.

Fat-Free version For a fat-free version, use fat-free cooking spray and **egg whites** only.

Millisecond Muffins

This basic muffin mix makes about 6 full-size muffins or 12 mini-muffins. With the Magic Bullet you can make three or four different varieties of muffins in less time than it takes to heat up the oven ... everyone gets their favorite!

Each muffin flavor starts with the Basic Muffin Mix recipe, you just add ingredients on top of that. We've found the easiest way to create multiple kinds of muffins with one batch of muffin mix is to create the Basic Muffin Mix in the *Tall Cup*, then transfer 1/3 or 1/2 of the basic mix to the *Short Cup*, add your additional ingredients, **Pulse** and pour into muffin tins.

Basic Muffin Mix
> 1 egg
> 1/2 cup milk
> 1 Tbs. vegetable oil
> 1 1/4 cups Bisquick (or any baking mix)
> 1/4 cup sugar

Before you start ... Preheat the oven to 350 degrees and grease a muffin tin, or line each cup with a paper muffin liner.

Then ... Add all of the ingredients, in the order listed above, into the *Tall Cup*.

And ... Mix until smooth.

If the ingredients ... are a little stubborn to mix, feel free to take the *Tall Cup* off the base and give it a good shake. Then put it back on and start blending again.

—Now move on to the specific muffin recipe you've chosen from the recipes below —

 A good way to test if your muffins, or bread, are done: stick a toothpick into the center of the muffin, or loaf; if batter sticks to it, then it isn't ready yet.

 Make a big batch of muffins To make more muffins, double or triple the ingredients and use the *Blender* attachment for mixing.

Blueberry Muffins

These fluffy, hot muffins are bursting at the seams with blueberry flavor. Just like Mom used to make, minus an hour of cooking time!

1/2 *Tall Cup* Basic Muffin Mix
   (See page 54)
good handful of fresh blueberries
2 Tbs. sugar (optional)
splash of milk

First ... Pour 1/2 of the Basic Muffin Mix into the *Short Cup*.
Then ... Add most of the blueberries and a splash of milk and **Pulse** until blended but still slightly textured.

Next ... Pour into muffin tins and add a few whole blueberries to the top.

Then ... Sprinkle a pinch of sugar over the top of each muffin (optional).

And ... Bake at 400 degrees for 15 minutes or until tops are golden brown.

 Tips ***Blueberry Bread*** To make Blueberry Bread, double or triple the ingredients and use the ***Blender*** attachment for mixing. Pour the ingredients into a greased loaf pan and cook at 400 degrees for 15-20 minutes, until golden brown on top.

Banana Nut Muffins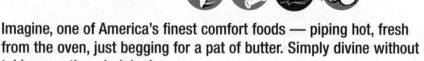

Imagine, one of America's finest comfort foods — piping hot, fresh from the oven, just begging for a pat of butter. Simply divine without taking any time. Indulge!

1/2 ***Tall Cup*** Basic Muffin Mix (See page 54)
1 banana (the riper the better)
1/4 cup shelled walnuts
pinch of sugar (optional)
splash of milk

First ... Pour 1/2 of the Basic Muffin Mix into the ***Short Cup***.

Then ... Add the banana, most of the walnuts and a splash of milk, and **Pulse** until blended but still slightly textured.

Next ... Pour into muffin tins and add a few big chunks of walnut to the top.

And ... Bake at 400 degrees for 15 minutes or until tops are golden brown.

 Tips ***Banana Nut Bread*** To make Banana Nut Bread, double or triple the ingredients and use the ***Blender*** attachment for mixing. Pour the ingredients into a greased loaf pan and cook at 400 degrees for 15-20 minutes, until golden brown on top.

Chocolate Chip Muffins

Warm, melted chocolate, what more needs to be said? These muffins melt in your mouth and practically make themselves. Enjoy!

1/2 *Tall Cup* Basic Muffin Mix (See page 54)
1/4 cup chocolate chips
splash of milk

First ... Pour 1/2 of the Basic Muffin Mix into the *Short Cup*.
Then ... Add in most of the chocolate chips and a splash of milk and **Pulse** until blended but still slightly textured.
Next ... Pour into muffin tins and add a few chocolate chips to the top.
And ... Bake at 400 degrees for 15 minutes or until tops are golden brown.

Tips *Chocolate Chip Bread* To make Chocolate Chip Bread, double or triple the ingredients and use the *Blender* attachment for mixing. Pour the ingredients into a greased loaf pan and cook at 400 degrees for 15-20 minutes, until golden brown on top.

In-An-Instant Cream Cheese Schmear

Ahh … whipped cream cheese, one of the finer things in life. A fabulous, easy breakfast, brunch or lunch delicacy. Bring on the bagels!

1 cup cream cheese
small splash of milk

Popular Add Ins
Chives
Sun dried tomatoes
Dill
Red Onion
Scallions
Basil
Smoked Salmon or Lox

Simply … Add the cream cheese and your favorite ingredients in to the *Tall Cup* and blend until smooth.

Cream cheese schmears are most often served with bagels. Some other tasty cream cheese treats are stuffed celery, just fill the center of a few celery stalks with cream cheese and cut into bite size pieces, or simply use the schmear as a veggie dip.

Soups

These delicious, all-natural, homemade soups are actually easier to make than canned soup: they take less time and make less mess. With the Magic Bullet you can mix, heat and eat your soup out of the same cup! You can even twist on a **Stay-fresh Re-sealable Lid** and bring your creamy, satisfying soups to work or school. Enjoy!

Brisk Broccoli Soup

Handed straight down from the broccoli gods, this recipe creates effortless piping hot, creamy, flavorful broccoli soup. It's remarkable!

> 1 cup broccoli florets
> 1 clove garlic
> 1/2 cup chicken stock
> 1/3 cup cream (milk, or nonfat yogurt)
> salt and pepper to taste

First ... Add broccoli, garlic and chicken stock to the **Tall Cup**.
Then ... Twist on the **Shaker/Steamer Top** and microwave for 2-3 minutes, until the broccoli is soft.
Next ... Open the cup, add cream and twist on the **Cross Blade**.
And ... Blend until you have a smooth souplike consistency.

Notes This recipe is for one bowl, or 2 cups, of soup. For more servings, just multiply each ingredient by the number of servings you want to create. For more than two bowl-sized servings, use the **Blender** attachment.

Tips **Fat-Free version.** Use fat-free plain yogurt or skim milk instead of cream.

Vegetarian version. Use vegetable broth instead of chicken broth to create a vegetarian version.

Kids will eat it. If you heat 1/4 cup of cheese with the broccoli, there is a very good chance your kids will gobble this up. You might want to play up the "cheese soup" part and play down the broccoli part.

Almost-Instant Asparagus Soup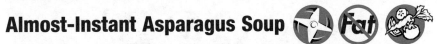

You'll have no soup to spare when you whip this fantastically flavorful, hearty soup. It's simply breathtaking.

1 cup asparagus tips (about 7-10 spears)
1 clove garlic
1/2 cup chicken stock
1/3 cup of cream (milk, nonfat yogurt)

First ... Add asparagus, garlic and chicken stock to the **Tall Cup**.
Then ... Twist on the **Shaker/Steamer Top** and microwave for 2-3 minutes, until the asparagus is soft.
Next ... Open cup and add cream, and twist on the **Cross Blade**.
And ... Blend until you have a smooth souplike consistency.

Notes This recipe is for one bowl, or 2 cups, of soup. For more servings, multiply each ingredient by the number of servings you want to create. For more than two bowl-sized servings, use the **Blender** attachment.

Tips **Make the most of your asparagus.** To make the most of your asparagus, don't use a knife to cut the ends off — snap the end of each stalk off with your hands, it will break off at exactly the point you want to use.
Fat-Free version. Use fat-free plain yogurt or skim milk instead of cream.

Vegetarian version. Use vegetable broth instead of chicken broth to create a vegetarian version.

Turbo Tomato Soup

Want to hear your kids beg for vegetables? This savory, homemade soup is sure to become a family favorite.

> 10-12 cherry tomatoes or 1 regular size tomato (about a cup)
> 1 clove garlic
> 1/2 cup chicken stock
> 1/3 cup cream (milk, nonfat yogurt)

First ... Add tomato, garlic and chicken stock to the ***Tall Cup***.
Then ... Twist on the ***Shaker/Steamer Top*** and microwave for 2-3 minutes, until the tomato is soft.
Next ... Open cup and add cream, and twist on the ***Cross Blade***.
And ... Blend until you have a smooth soup-like consistency.

This recipe is for one bowl, or 2 cups, of soup. For more servings, just multiply each ingredient by the number of servings you want to create. For more than two bowl-sized servings, use the ***Blender*** attachment.

Fat-Free version. Use fat-free plain yogurt or skim milk instead of cream. ***Vegetarian version.*** Use vegetable broth instead of chicken broth to create a vegetarian version.

Gruel-less Gazpacho

This elegant and tasty traditional Italian soup is a sure crowd-pleaser. Absolutely perfect for a brunch appetizer. If you're looking to impress your guests, make this gazpacho and it's a slam dunk.

> 1/2 red pepper
> 1-2 cloves garlic
> 1 cup chicken stock
> splash of red wine vinegar
> 1/4 of a hothouse (English) cucumber
> sprig of fresh chopped parsley

First ... Add all of the ingredients in the order listed to the *Tall Cup* and twist on the *Cross Blade*.

Then ... Pulse (see **Pulse** Technique on Page 15) until the consistency is smooth but still has some texture.

This recipe is for two good-sized bowls of soup, or 4 cups of soup.

Gazpacho is best served cold. For a fabulously fancy appetizer, place chilled, cooked baby shrimp in the bottom of small cocktail cups and pour gazpacho over the top.

Vegetarian version. Use vegetable broth instead of chicken broth to create a vegetarian version.

Use as a dip. This can also be used as a tasty chip dip.

Soups and Sandwiches

Sandwiches

Tired of the "same old, same old" for lunch? Sick of spending your hard-earned money on overpriced lunches because you don't have the time to pack a lunch? Thanks to the Magic Bullet, now you can have gourmet, transportable, delicious, even fat-free sandwiches that take seconds to make, and cost a fraction of what you pay for takeout.

Six-Second Chicken Salad

In all honesty, we had forgotten how simply divine classic chicken salad can be. The nuts and apple create a sandwich spread that is irresistible.

    1/4 of a cored apple (about 1/4 cup)
    slice of onion (about 1/8 cup)
    1 cup cooked chicken (leftovers, even luncheon meat)
    2 Tbs. walnuts
    1-2 Tbs. mayonnaise

First ... Add the ingredients in the order they appear to the **Short Cup** and twist on the Cross Blade.

Then use ... the quick **Pulse** technique (Page 15) to chop and mix the ingredients. Just press down on the cup and release the pressure immediately, pause and let the ingredients settle (or use the **Tap** technique on Page 17), then quickly **Pulse** again until you've reached a good consistency.

Remember to ... Apply a bit of counter-clockwise pressure to the cup to keep it from **Locking On.** (See **Pulsing** techniques on Page 15)

Then ... Spread between two slices of bread and enjoy.

Notes
Even the Magic Bullet can't defy the laws of physics, so if you've overloaded the cup, or if your chicken salad ingredients are too dense for the ingredients at the top of the cup to reach the blade, we recommend you try the **Shake** or **Tap** techniques on Page 16 and 17. If it's really thick, scoop out the finished chicken salad that has accumulated at the bottom, put it in a bowl, then continue **Pulsing** the remaining ingredients. Once everything is chopped, you can add it all back together in the cup and give it a quick **Pulse** to mix everything together.

Serving Suggestion
Chicken salad is very versatile. Feel free to add other things into your list of ingredients. Try sprinkling in a little nutmeg or cinnamon. Serve on toast, or add a scoop on top of a mixed green salad. Have you ever seen a more satisfying way to eat leftovers? Bon appetit!

Tips
Fat-Free version. Use fat-free chicken broth and fat-free ranch dressing, or fat-free plain yogurt, instead of mayonnaise for a zesty fat-free lunch or dinner.
Stuffed tomatoes or peppers. Hollow out the inside of a tomato or pepper and fill with chicken salad ... a bread-free, delicious and attractive lunch.

To create **Mick's Curry Chicken Salad**, skip the apples and walnuts and add a dash or two of curry powder.

Egg Salad Express

Delicious, flavorful egg salad without the slicing and dicing — how wonderful! A quick and tasty lunch that parents and kids will thoroughly enjoy.

> 2 hard-boiled eggs
> 1 stalk celery
> slice of onion (about 1/8 cup)
> 1-2 Tbs. mayonnaise
> pinch of mustard powder (optional)

Before you begin ... Break the celery stalks in half and pull to remove as much of the celery string as possible.
Then ... Add the ingredients in the order they appear to the ***Short Cup*** and twist on the ***Cross Blade***.
Pulse using the quick Pulse technique ... just press down on the cup and release the pressure immediately, pause and let the ingredients settle, than quickly **Pulse** again until you've reached a good consistency.
And serve.

Notes Spice things up by adding a little sweet pickle relish, or add a dab of Dijon mustard to your ingredients before you blend. Sprinkle a little paprika over the top and grab yourself a napkin because this sandwich isn't going to be around long enough to touch the plate!

Tips ***Fat-Free version.*** Use mustard and a splash of chicken or veggie broth instead of mayonnaise for a tasty, fat-free version.

Stuffed tomatoes or peppers. Hollow out the inside of a tomato or pepper and fill with egg salad ... a bread-free, delicious, attractive lunch.

Lickety-Split Deviled Ham

This stunningly delicious sandwich spread is appealing to both adults and kids and couldn't be easier, or quicker, to make. Its smoky, mustard flavor is unbelievably delicious, just perfect for sandwich platters.

> 1 1/2 cups cooked smoked ham (or fat free smoked turkey ham)
> 1/3 cup chicken broth
> 1 Tbs. Dijon mustard
> slice of onion (about 1/8 cup)

First ... Add the ingredients in the order they appear to the **Short Cup** and twist on the **Cross Blade.**
Then use... the quick **Pulse** technique (Page 15) to chop and mix the ingredients. Just press down on the cup and release the pressure immediately, pause and let the ingredients settle (or use the **Tap** technique on page 17), then quickly **Pulse** again until you reach a good consistency.
Then serve!

Serve sandwich-style on bread, or **Pulse** until smooth and serve it paté-style as a spread for crackers, or slices of crusty Italian or French bread.

Pinwheel Sandwiches. Deviled ham is perfect for pinwheel sandwiches, just spread the ham and some cream cheese evenly over lavash bread (or tortillas) and roll up into a log. Slice into 1/2-3/4-inch rounds (you may need a toothpick to hold the wheels together) for a lovely lunchtime treat.

Pasta Sauces

Each of these pasta sauces is so quick and easy that everyone can have their favorite. In less time than it takes to heat up a jar of sauce on the stove top, you can whip up a batch of creamy Alfredo Sauce, a serving of mouth-watering Pesto Sauce and a rich, hearty Meat Sauce. As if that isn't enough, cleanup is a breeze. You mix and heat in the same cup. Just throw the cup in the dishwasher and you're done. No cutting boards, pots or pans! Hooray!

Im"meat"iate Spaghetti Sauce (Marinara)

Whether you want to start from scratch, or create a mouth-watering sauce from leftovers, this meat sauce recipe is for you. Every morsel is bursting with flavor.

> 1/4 cup chicken broth
> 10-12 cherry tomatoes or 1 (quartered) regular size tomato (about a cup)
> 1 boiler onion or 1/4 of a regular sized onion (about 1/4 cup)
> 2 Tbs. red wine (optional)
> 2 Tbs. tomato paste
> 2 cloves garlic
> 2 sprigs basil
> 1/4 cup raw hamburger, steak or turkey (see Notes for using cooked meat)
> pinch of Italian seasoning (optional)
> salt and pepper to taste

First ... Add all ingredients in the order they are listed to the *Tall Cup* and twist on the *Cross Blade*. **Pulse using the quick Pulse (Page 7) technique** ... Just press down on the cup and release the pressure immediately, pause and let the ingredients settle, than quickly **Pulse** again until you've reached a good consistency.

Then ... Twist off *Cross Blade* and twist on a *Shaker/Steamer Top*.
And ... Place cup the in microwave and cook on high for 8 to 10
minutes, until the meat is cooked. Every microwave is different, so
keep an eye on things after 7 minutes; if it looks like your liquid is
starting to dry up, use an oven mitt to take the sauce out and give it
a stir, and heat for about 30 more seconds. (You may want to add a
little water or wine).
Stir ... and serve over hot pasta.

Cooking the meat right in the sauce gives it an unusual texture,
although the taste is out of this world because all of the flavors
are blended together. If the texture bothers you, microwave the
meat in the Bullet cup first, then make as usual. This recipe
makes two good-sized servings of sauce. For larger batches, double
the ingredients and use the blender attachment.

Add a little fresh Parmesan cheese to the top of your piping hot
pasta dish! Just add a chunk of Parmesan to the *Short Cup*
and twist on the *Cross Blade*. Chop until the consistency is a
coarse powder. Twist on a *Shaker/Steamer Top*, sprinkle over
the top of your pasta and enjoy!

Use leftover meat If you have leftover cooked meat ... follow
the same instructions as above but replace the raw hamburger
with your leftover chicken, steak, burgers, sausage, pork —
whatever you've got. You'll only need to microwave your sauce
for about 6 minutes.
Make Bolognese sauce If you want **Bolognese Sauce**, just add 1/2
cup of heavy cream and another splash of red wine to cooked sauce
and **Pulse** one or two times.

Dinners

It's Ready Already Alfredo

Whoever Alfredo is, we need to hand it to him. This creamy, rich, traditional Italian sauce has been around for hundreds of years for a good reason: it's amazing!

- 1/4 cup of heavy cream
- 2 Tbs. of butter
- 1 - 2 cloves of garlic
- 1/2 cup Parmesan cheese
- 3 sprigs of fresh parsley
- salt and pepper to taste

First ... Add all ingredients in the order they are listed to the *Tall Cup* and twist on the *Cross Blade*.

Then ... Blend everything together until smooth.

Next you... Twist off the *Cross Blade* and twist on the *Shaker/Steamer Top*.

Then cook ... in the microwave on high for 1-2 minutes, until the sauce is heated thoroughly.

And Then: Twist on the *Flat Blade* and **Pulse** the sauce 3-4 times.

Stir ... and serve over hot pasta.

Notes
This recipe makes one good-sized serving of sauce. Double or triple the ingredients and use the *Tall Cup* to make more servings.

Serving Suggestion
Add a little fresh Parmesan cheese to the top of your piping hot pasta dish! Just add a chunk of Parmesan to the *Short Cup* and twist on the *Cross Blade*. Chop until the consistency is a coarse powder. Sprinkle over the top and enjoy!

Presto It's Pesto

Rich, flavorful and hearty, this simple, quick pesto sauce is a surefire treat for even the most gourmet of palates.

> 10-12 fresh basil leaves
> 2 Tbs. of pine nuts
> 2 Tbs. extra-virgin olive oil
> 1 1/2 tsp. coarse salt (optional)
> 1-2 cloves of garlic
> 1 small chunk Parmesan cheese

First ... Add all ingredients in the order they appear into the **Tall Cup**.
Then ... Screw on the **Cross Blade** and **Pulse** until the pesto has the consistency of a slightly grainy paste.
Next ... Twist off the **Cross Blade** and twist on the **Shaker/Steamer Top**.
And ... Place the cup in microwave and cook on high for 2 to 3 minutes, until the sauce is heated thoroughly.
Stir ... and serve over hot pasta.

 This recipe makes one good-sized serving of sauce. Double or triple the ingredients and use the **Tall Cup** to make more servings. If you want a slightly thinner sauce, feel free to add more oil until you've achieved the desired thickness.

 Add a little fresh Parmesan cheese to the top of your piping hot pasta dish! Just add a chunk of Parmesan to the **Short Cup** and twist on the **Cross Blade**. Chop until the consistency is a coarse powder. Twist on a **Shaker/Steamer Top** and sprinkle it over your pesto ... enjoy!

 Pesto dip. Pesto also makes a great dip. Serve hot, or at room temperature, with sliced Italian or French bread.

Dinners

Super Easy Macaroni & Cheese

Mm, melted cheese … need we say more? Macaroni and cheese isn't the world's most popular comfort food for no reason, it's sensational. And with the Magic Bullet, it's effortless. Kids will gobble this dish up!

    1/4 cup cheddar (or Velveeta) cheese
    splash of heavy cream (or milk)

First … Add cheese and cream to the *Short Cup*.
Then … Microwave on high for 1-2 minutes, until the cheese is fully melted.
Remove the cup from the microwave … using an oven mitt, twist on the *Flat Blade* and **Pulse** 3-4 times.
Pour … over hot macaroni noodles and serve.

 This recipe makes one good-sized serving of sauce. Double or triple the ingredients and use the *Tall Cup* to make more servings.

 Sneak in veggies. Kids love this macaroni and cheese so much that slipping some vegetables in post-microwave but pre-mixing is worth a shot. Pop a tomato or some steamed broccoli in there. You'll be amazed at how forgiving this recipe can be.

Desserts

Finally a way to make desserts without messing up the entire kitchen! From rich and creamy cheesecake to fat-free fruit sorbets, these recipes will please the palate, satisfy that sweet tooth and get you out of the kitchen in no time.

Cheesecake

Delicious cheesecake has never been easier. In seconds, you can prepare the fluffiest, creamiest cheesecake to ever touch a fork!

   1 (8 oz.) package cream cheese
   2 eggs
   1/2 cup sugar
   1 tsp. vanilla
   1 graham cracker crust

Before you get started ... Preheat the oven to 350 degrees.
First ... Add all the ingredients (except crust) to the *Tall Cup* and mix until smooth.
Then ... Pour the ingredients into the graham cracker crust.
And ... Bake at 350 degrees for 20-25 minutes (until set).

Fruit toppings are always a scrumptious way to top a cheesecake. To make **Strawberry Cheesecake**, or **Blueberry Cheesecake**, fill the *Short Cup* up 3/4 of the way with your fresh strawberries or blueberries, add 1-2 tablespoons of sugar, and blend until you achieve a chunky syrup consistency. Pour that over the top of the cooled cheesecake (at least an hour in the refrigerator), then add a layer of sliced strawberries, or whole blueberries, to the top. Chill for a few hours, then serve.

Tips ***Totally easy cherry topping*** Just let your cheesecake cool for at least an hour in the refrigerator, then add a can of cherry topping to the top of it. Totally delicious and virtually effortless **Cherry Cheesecake!**

Chocolate Mousse

You will think you died and went to Heaven ... all for about 4 seconds worth of effort. This rich and tantalizingly decadent dessert will impress everyone who tastes it.

    1/4 cup heavy cream
    2 Tbs. chocolate syrup

First ... Add the ingredients to the *Short Cup* and blend until smooth.
Then ... Serve.

This makes one serving. For more servings, double or triple the recipe.

Using the *Flat Blade*, grind a few chocolate chips up in the *Short Cup*. Twist on a *Shaker/Steamer Top* and sprinkle a little on the top of your chocolate mousse. You can also whip some cream (Page 24) and add a dollop to the top of each serving of chocolate mousse.

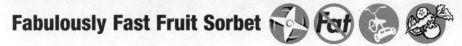

Fabulously Fast Fruit Sorbet

A healthy, refreshing dessert in seconds! Your kids will think it's ice cream and beg for this all-natural, sugar-free delight day after day.

> 1 cup of your favorite frozen fruit (we love mixed berries)
> 2-3 tablespoons water (or fruit juice, or your favorite liqueur)

First ... Add ingredients to the *Short Cup* and blend until smooth.
Then ... Serve.

 To reach your ideal consistency, you may want to add more water or fruit juice to the frozen fruit.

 For a fancy brunch or party dessert, make a variety of flavors (blueberry, strawberry, mango) and pour the different flavors into cocktail glasses. For an impressive visual display, add flavors with contrasting colors in the same cup.

Six-Second Milkshakes

> splash of milk
> 1 1/2 cup vanilla ice cream
> chocolate syrup

First ... Add all of the ingredients, in the order they appear, to the Tall Cup (or Party Mug) and mix until smooth.
Then ... Serve immediately

If you like to drink your milkshakes with a straw, add more milk to thin it out and blend a little more. If you want to make a large batch of milkshakes, double or triple the ingredients and use the Magic Bullet *Blender*.

For a **Blueberry Milkshake** leave out the chocolate and add a hand full of fresh or frozen blueberries.

For a **Strawberry Milkshake** add a handful of fresh or frozen strawberries.

For a **Chocolate Monster Milkshake** use chocolate ice cream and add in your favorite bite-size candy bar.

For **Mimi's Chocolate Chocolate Mint Milkshake** add 1/4 of a chocolate bar and two starlight mint candies.

For a **Bullet Blizzard** add tiny colored chocolate candies to the regular Milkshake recipe.

For a **North Pole** add a mint patty to the regular Milkshake recipe.

Make 100% pure and natural, homemade baby food in just seconds with the Magic Bullet. Now for a fraction of the price of store-bought baby food, you can know exactly what ingredients your baby is eating. Create your own special blends, use organic fruits and vegetables — it's all up to you. Your tiny one is going to gobble this food up with a smile.

Carrot Baby Food

1 cup baby carrots
splash of water

First... Toss baby carrots and a splash of water to the *Short Cup*, twist on a *Shaker/Steamer Top* and steam the carrots until tender.
Next ... Strain off most of the extra water. The more water you keep, the thinner the consistency. For younger babies, keep a tablespoon or so of water. For bigger kids, drain almost all of the water. You can always add more to thin it out.
Then ... Twist on *Cross Blade* and blend until you've achieved a smooth puree.
And ... Let cool and serve.

Chicken and Rice Baby Food

1/2 cup cooked chicken
1/2 cup cooked rice
splash of water or chicken stock

First ... Place ingredients in the *Short Cup* and twist on the *Cross Blade*.
Then ... Blend until smooth.
And ... Heat until slightly warm and serve.

Leftover Special

Basically throw any leftovers you can find in the *Short Cup* and blend until smooth — your baby will love it!

Coffee Drinks

Now you can make gourmet coffee drinks at home for a fraction of the price you'd pay at a coffee shop. Why wait in line only to spend your hard-earned money when you can use your Magic Bullet to create great-tasting warm coffee brews and ice blended drinks right at home?

Café Mocha

All the comfort of hot chocolate with an espresso kick, rolled into one piping hot cuppa joe that is sure to please.

> milk
> fresh hot coffee
> 3-4 Tbs. chocolate syrup (or cocoa powder)
> 1-2 tsp. sugar (optional)

Start by ... grinding your own dark roasted beans using the *Flat Blade* (See Grinding Coffee section on page 20). The finer the grind the stronger the coffee, so blend into a coarse sand texture for lighter brews or a fine powder for strong coffee.
Then ... Brew a pot of coffee.
Now ... Fill 1/4 of the *Tall Cup* with milk and blend with the *Cross Blade* to make it frothy.
And ... Microwave the milk on high for 35-45 seconds (be careful not to let the milk foam up out of the cup ... stop it before it hits the top of the cup).
Next ... Open the cup and add the chocolate syrup, then fill the *Tall Cup* just about to the top with coffee and **Pulse** 3 or 4 times.
And ... Pour into cups and serve.

Notes This makes two servings. For one serving, reduce each ingredient by a half. For four servings, simply double the ingredients.

Tips

Whipped cream topping Add a dollop of whipped cream to the top of each cup. Just add heavy cream to the ***Short Cup***, and whip with the ***Flat Blade*** (See Whipping Cream on page 24).

Cappuccino

This simple classic has the perfect coffee-to-milk ratio. It's espresso at its finest, and oh, that delicious foam!

2 coffee cups filled with hot espresso (or hot coffee)
milk
2 pinches powdered cocoa or cinnamon (optional)

Start by ... grinding your own dark roasted beans using the ***Flat Blade***. The finer the grind the stronger the coffee, so blend into a coarse sand texture for lighter brews or a fine powder for strong coffee (See Grinding Coffee section on page 20).
Then ... Brew a pot of coffee.
Now ... Fill the ***Short Cup*** full of milk and blend with the ***Cross Blade*** for 5-10 seconds.
And ... Microwave the milk on high for 35-45 seconds (be careful not to let the milk foam up out of the cup — stop it before it hits the top of the cup).
Next ... Pour coffee into 2 cups while you let the milk settle for a bit.
Then ... Pour the thinner steamed milk into the coffee, then scoop out dollops of the foamy milk and let it ride on the top.
If you want ... Sprinkle each drink with a pinch of cocoa or cinnamon and serve.

Notes

This makes two servings. For one serving, reduce each ingredient by a half. For four servings, simply double the ingredients.

Tips

Add a little sugar. Feel free to add a little sugar to your cappuccino if that's the way you like it.

Igloo Espresso

Chill out with this cool, refreshing drink. It will put a kick in your step and a smile on your face ... enjoy!

> fresh espresso (or leftover coffee)
> ice
> whipping cream

First ... Fill the *Tall Cup* with ice and add as much espresso as you can fit.

And ... Mix with the *Cross Blade* until smooth and pour into serving glasses.

If you want ... Add whipping cream to the *Short Cup* and blend with the *Flat Blade* for about 5 seconds (you'll hear when it's ready).

Then ... Pour whipped cream over the top of the espresso and serve.

This makes two servings. For one serving, reduce each ingredient by a half. For four servings, simply double the ingredients

Tips

Add a little sugar. Feel free to add a little sugar to your Igloo Espresso if that's the way you like it.

Iced Mocha

A chilly, refreshing version of the hot mocha drink. A perfect pick-me-up on a hot summer day.

- 2 cups coffee
- 2-3 Tbs. chocolate syrup (or cocoa powder)
- 2 cups milk
- 1-2 tsp. sugar (optional)
- 1 1/2-2 cups ice

First ... Brew a pot of coffee (or use leftover coffee).

Next ... Fill the *Tall Cup* with ice. Add the chocolate syrup, milk, sugar, then fill the cup to the top with coffee and mix with the *Cross Blade* until smooth.

And ... Pour mixture into 2 coffee cups.

If you want ... Add whipping cream to the *Short Cup* and blend with the *Flat Blade* for about 5 seconds. Add to the top of the coffee mixtures and serve.

 This makes two servings. For one serving, reduce each ingredient by a half. For four servings, simply double the ingredients.

Irish Coffee

Designed to endure those long, rainy overcast nights in Ireland, this warm drink is the perfect blend of java and juice, a real treat for the taste buds.

> 2 tablespoons orange juice
> 2 teaspoons lemon juice
> strong hot coffee
> 1/2 cup whipping cream
> 2 shots of Irish Whiskey (optional)

Start by ... grinding your own coffee beans using the *Flat Blade*. The finer the grind the stronger the coffee, so blend into a coarse sand texture for lighter brews, or a fine powder for strong coffee.
Then ... Add the orange juice and lemon juice in the *Tall Cup*, then fill the rest of the cup to the top with coffee.
Next ... Add whipping cream to the *Short Cup* and blend with the *Flat Blade* for about 5 seconds.
Then ... Pour the coffee mixture into 2 coffee cups, add whiskey and top with whipped cream.

Notes

This makes two servings. For one serving, just reduce each ingredient by a half. For four servings, double the ingredients

Coffee Drinks

The Magic Bullet is perfect for creating delicious, satisfying, frosty smoothies and meal replacement drinks. The best part is that you blend your ingredients and drink your smoothie out of the very same dishwasher-friendly cup ... no mess! Plus, the power of the Magic Bullet distributes flavor in such a way that every molecule of your smoothie is bursting with flavor.

Strawberry Banana Smoothie

A deliciously satisfying, fruity drink that is perfect for any time of the day.

> handful of fresh or frozen strawberries
> 1 banana
> 1 cup ice
> splash of orange juice

First ... Add all ingredients to the *Tall Cup* or *Party Mug* and twist on the *Cross Blade*.
Then ... Lock On and mix until smooth.
Next ... Drink up!

You can leave the tops on the strawberries; that's where a lot of the nutrients are.

Mixed Berry Smoothie

This tasty smoothie is jam-packed with fresh berry flavor. This is one your kids will love.

> handful of fresh or frozen mixed berries
> 1 banana
> 1 cup ice
> splash of orange juice

First ... Add all ingredients to the *Tall Cup* or *Party Mug*.
Then ... **Lock On** and mix until smooth.
Next ... Serve.

Choco-Berry Protein Smoothie Meal Replacement

This chocolate and blueberry flavor combination is worthy of celebration; how can something so healthy taste so good?

> 1/2 cup milk (fat-free for healthiest)
> 1 handful of fresh or frozen blueberries
> ice cubes
> 2 (or more) scoops chocolate protein powder
> 1/2 medium-sized banana

First ... Fill the *Tall Cup* of *Party Mug* halfway with ice.
Then ... Add the remaining ingredients to the *Tall Cup* or *Party Mug*.
Next ... **Lock On** and mix until smooth.
    And ... Serve.

Notes: This recipe makes one serving. For more than one serving, multiply each ingredient by the number of servings you want to make and use the blender attachment for mixing. This is a basic meal replacement drink; feel free to adjust the ingredients to fit your specific diet plan.

Tips: A lot of the popular 5-6 meal a day diet plans call for meals and snacks of lean protein and complex carbs, these meal replacement drinks are a tasty, easy way to lose weight!

There is something about freshly squeezed fruit and vegetable juices — they're good for the soul. And now with the Magic Bullet, it's easy to enjoy fresh juice every day of the week.

Please enjoy some of our favorites, then experiment to your heart's content. Your perfect blend of fruits or vegetables — or both — is out there. You just have to find it. When you do, feel free to share it with the rest of us by posting it on the Magic Bullet website at www.BuyTheBullet.com

Fresh Orange Juice

Straight from the heavens, this 100% pure, fresh orange juice is absolutely divine and so easy to make, you can have it every morning of the week.

   3 quartered ripe oranges (peeled)

Before you get started ... Assemble the *Juicer* (Page 29) and make sure your ingredients are within arms reach and sized to fit into the pop-top of the *Blender Lid*.
Then ... Put the Magic Bullet into **Lock On** mode.
And ... Add the oranges into the *Extractor* and push down with the plunger.
Then ... Pour the juice into a glass (keep the lid of the blender on while pouring).

 Never run the Magic Bullet for more than a minute, it can cause permanent damage to the motor. If you do overheat the motor and it stops, unplug the *Power Base* and let it rest for a few hours before attempting to use it again.

Fresh Pineapple Juice

Refreshing, tangy 100% natural pineapple juice … life doesn't get much better!

1/3 of a fresh pineapple (the rind is ok)

Before you get started … Assemble the *Juicer* (Page 29) and make sure your ingredients are within arms reach and sized to fit into the pop-top of the *Blender Lid*.
Then … Put the Magic Bullet into **Lock On** mode.
And … Add the pineapple into the *Extractor* and push down with the plunger.
Then … Pour the juice into a glass (keep the lid of the blender on while pouring).

Caution

If the blade stops in Lock On mode, unplug the Magic Bullet immediately. Sometimes, especially when the motor is coming up to speed, a hard ingredient, such as a carrot chunk, can get stuck in the blade. If the blade stops, UNPLUG THE MAGIC BULLET IMMEDIATELY. Give the Bullet a shake to jostle the ingredients, then start again. If it doesn't start to blend, unplug, take the blade/cup off and give the ingredients a good shake to unclog the blade. If the blade still seems obstructed, twist off the blade and carefully (it's sharp) spin the blade manually. Once the blade will spin, plug the Magic Bullet back in and try again — you should be good to go.

Notes

Never run the Magic Bullet for more than one minute, it can cause permanent damage to the motor. If you do overheat the motor and it stops, unplug the *Power Base* and let it rest for a few hours before attempting to use it again.

Energy Cocktail

This hearty, rich, energy drink is chock full of antioxidants and flavor. The perfect blend to start your day.

> 2-3 chunks of watermelon (about 6 inches long)
> 2 chunks of pineapple (about 6 inches long)
> 1 beet
> a handful of fresh spinach
> 3-4 broccoli florettes

Before you get started ... Make sure your ingredients are sized to fit into the pop top of the *Blender Lid*.
Next ... put the Bullet into **Lock On mode**.
Then ... add the ingredients into the *Extractor* in the order they are listed, using the plunger to push the ingredients in to the blade.
When its ready ... Pour the juice into a glass (keep the lid of the Blender on while pouring.
And ... serve over ice.

Never run the Magic Bullet for more than one minute, it can cause permanent damage to the motor. If you do overheat the motor and it stops, unplug the *Power Base* and let it rest for a few hours before attempting to use it again.

7 Minute Cocktail Party

Ready to throw a Bullet Bash? Follow these steps and you'll be ready to show your guests the time of their lives, Magic Bullet style.

The Seven-Minute Cocktail Party

How about a snazzy little cocktail party to catch up with some old friends? Here is a menu that is perfect for an intimate evening get-together for six.

Guests Arrive to:
Before-You-Know-It Bean Dip With Warm Pita Triangles
Hallelujah Hummus With Warm Pita Triangles

Cocktails:
Mystic Martinis
Boulevard Bellinis

Appetizers:
Suddenly Stuffed Mushrooms
Garlic Bread Rounds With Pesto Dip

Coffee:
Irish Coffee

SHOPPING LIST

Produce Section
   1 medium onion
   10 cloves garlic
   18-24 large mushrooms
   fresh spinach
   1 package fresh basil leaves

Frozen Foods Section
   frozen peaches

Spices/Cooking/Canned Fruits and Vegetables Section
coarse salt
cayenne pepper (optional)
balsamic vinegar
jarred roasted red peppers
paprika
tahini (sesame paste)
olive oil
chicken or vegetable broth
pine nuts
sugar
cocktail olives
cocktail onions
1 (14 oz.) can black beans
1 (14 oz.) can chickpeas (garbanzo beans)

Beverage Section
1/4 pound dark roast coffee
orange juice
lemon juice (or juice of one lemon)
whiskey
vodka or gin
dry vermouth
champagne
peach schnapps
lemon-lime soda
2 lbs. ice

Bread Section
3 packages pita bread
2 large French baguettes

Dairy Section
1/2 cup whipping cream
Parmesan cheese

Ricotta cheese
sour cream
butter or margarine

Non-Food Item Needs
20 -30 cocktail napkins
20-30 appetizer plates
6 martini glasses
6 coffee cups
toothpicks (for martini olives)
2 baking sheets
1 serving platter for dips and pitas
1 serving platter for mushrooms
1 serving platter for bread and pesto dip

ONE HOUR BEFORE PARTY TIME

Step 1: Make up a batch of Black Bean Dip. Follow the recipe on Page 35 and then chill in the refrigerator.

Step 2: Make up a batch of Hummus. Follow the recipe on Page 34 and then chill in the refrigerator.

Step 3: Make up a double batch of Stuffed Mushrooms. Follow the recipe on Page 39, lay the mushrooms out on a cookie sheet and then chill in the refrigerator.

Step 4: Slice the baguette into 1/3-inch rounds, spread on garlic bread mixture (Page 41) and lay the rounds out on a cookie sheet.

Step 5: Mix up a batch of Pesto Sauce (triple the recipe on Page 70) but don't heat it yet, store in the refrigerator.

Step 6: Make sure your serving platters are clean and ready to go and cut up pita bread into triangles.

Step 7: Arrange the napkins and plates near your serving area.

Step 8: Go freshen up.

TEN MINUTES BEFORE PARTY TIME

Step 1: Place vodka or gin, vermouth, olives, champagne, peach schnapps, frozen peaches, lemon-lime soda and a bowl of ice within arms reach of the Magic Bullet.

Step 2: Pour the Hummus and Black Bean Dip into their serving trays, add the pita triangles to the tray and place in serving area near the napkins and plates.

Step 3: Go relax and wait for your guests.

PARTY TIME

Step 1: As guests arrive, offer them a martini (page 48) or bellini (page 47) and show them where the dips are.

Step 2: Show off the Magic Bullet. Let your friends give it a whirl.

Step 3: Enjoy yourself.

30 MINUTES IN

Step 1: Preheat the oven to 350 degrees.

45 MINUTES IN

Step 1: Place the Stuffed Mushrooms and bread slices in the oven. When they are just about done, heat up the Pesto Sauce. Then serve your guests the Stuffed Mushrooms and Bread with Pesto Sauce spread.

AN HOUR AND 1/2 TO 2 HOURS IN

Step 1: Brew a pot of coffee and ask your guests if anyone is interested in an Irish Coffee (the whiskey is optional).

Step 2: Follow Irish Coffee recipe on Page 81 and serve to guests.

INDEX

Fat-Free Dishes

Vegetarian Dishes

INDEX

Kid-Friendly

INDEX

www.BuyTheBullet.com

Check out the official Magic Bullet website by going to www.BuyTheBullet.com where you can order the Magic Bullet, learn about product accessories and more. You can submit your Magic Bullet recipes and Bullet Bash pictures -- we'll consider posting them on the site! We even have a suggestion box where you can recommend product enhancements and accessories, as well as what you'd like to see on the BuyTheBullet site.

Limited Warranty

MAGIC BULLET ONE-YEAR LIMITED WARRANTY

At Homeland Housewares, we take pride in our products. We go out of our way to make products of superior quality and craftsmanship, products designed to meet or exceed the demands placed on them through everyday use. Because of this commitment to quality, we warrant the Magic Bullet to be free of defects for one full year. Here's the deal: If your Magic Bullet stops operating to your satisfaction due to defects in materials or workmanship, we'll gladly repair it or replace it for free (excluding shipping and handling charges). For warranty service, simply call our customer service department @ **800-423-4248** and we'll be glad to help you. At Homeland Housewares, your complete satisfaction is our daily goal (hey, we know what it's like to be the customer!).

Homeland Housewares warrants that the Magic Bullet is free of defects in materials and workmanship for one year from the date of purchase. This warranty is valid only in accordance with the conditions set forth below:

1. Normal wear and tear are not covered by this warranty. This warranty applies to consumer use only, and is void when the product is used in a commercial or institutional setting.

2. This warranty extends only to the original consumer purchaser and is not transferable. In addition, proof of purchase must be demonstrated. This warranty is void if the product has been subject to accident, misuse, abuse, improper maintenance or repair, or unauthorized modification.

3. This limited warranty is the only written or express warranty given by Homeland Housewares. Any implied warranties on the product (including but not limited to any implied warranties of merchantability or fitness for a particular purpose) are limited in duration to the duration of this warranty. Some states do not allow limitations on how long an implied warranty lasts, so the above limitation may not apply to you.

4. Repair or replacement of the product (or, if repair or replacement is not feasible, a refund of the purchase price) is the exclusive remedy of the consumer under this warranty. Homeland Housewares shall not be liable for any incidental or consequential damages for breach of this warranty or any implied warranty on this product. Some states do not allow the exclusion or limitation of incidental or consequential damages, so the above limitation or exclusion may not apply to you.

5. This warranty gives you specific legal rights, and you may also have other rights which vary from state to state.

Recipe Favorites: